the little book of

FLIRTING

the little book of

FLIRTING
seven days to being a great flirt

Peta Heskell

Element
An Imprint of HarperCollins*Publishers*
77–85 Fulham Palace Road,
Hammersmith, London W6 8JB

ELEMENT

and *Element*
are trademarks of HarperCollins*Publishers* Ltd

First published by Element 2002

3 5 7 9 10 8 6 4 2

© Peta Heskell 2002

Peta Heskell asserts the moral right to
be identified as the author of this work

A catalogue record of this book is
available from the British Library

ISBN 0 00 714663 9

Printed and bound in Great Britain by
Martins The Printers Ltd, Berwick Upon Tweed

Flirt Coach:

Communication tips for friendship, love and professional success

DEDICATION

To everyone who has the courage to leap into life's adventure and go for it.

A mega thanks to all my clients, participants of the playshops and friends who made it possible for me to do my work and spread a little sunshine in the world. Keep shining.

CONTENTS

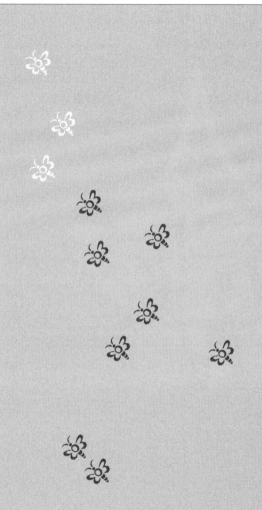

Introduction

What do we mean by 'flirting' anyway?

Let's begin by redefining the word 'flirting'. Remember, if we didn't redefine things as we went along we'd all still be hunting for our meat and living in caves. Flirting comes from the old French word *fleurter*, meaning 'to flower'. Here are a few modern definitions from participants in my flirting classes:

- ♥ Flirting is about fun, connecting with and getting to know people.

- ♥ Flirting is a way of showing people you are interested in them.

⊙ Flirting is about giving compliments, smiling and making people happy.

⊙ Flirting is like a butterfly that flutters past in all its beauty, and when we try to catch it, it flies away leaving us wanting more . . .

⊙ Flirting is making yourself so attractive that people can't resist you.

⊙ Flirting is being able to break down people's barriers and make contact.

⊙ Flirting is a harmless entertaining diversion that you can choose to take further if you wish.

introduction

Here's a mnemonic that sums up flirting for me:

Feeling good about yourself.

Liking other people.

Interest in others makes YOU interesting.

Rapport and resonance.

Talking their language.

Initiating conversation.

'No' means move on to the next. No, next, no, next! Bingo! Yes!

Giving great voice and loosening up your body.

Flirting isn't just restricted to interaction with the opposite sex. It's also useful in social and work situations. Your style of flirting can range from simply social to strongly sexual. Great flirting, when done appropriately and with a friendly go-for-it attitude, is the gateway to more romance, deeper friendships, enhanced professional relationships and a definite feel-good sensation for you and people you flirt with.

introduction

Flirting is feeling great about yourself
and resonating this to the world so that
the right people are drawn to you –

irresistibly!

The best flirts do it with everyone!

This book is about how to be the kind of person who can flirt with anyone they choose! My friend Lesley is like that. She ran a business for 25 years, flirting with everyone. To this day she flirts with elderly people, children, babies, men and women. She flirts saucily with men she fancies and kindly with men she doesn't. She enjoys a joke and she can be really raunchy *and* very gentle. At the age of 49 she still has men chasing after her and she's been happily married for 26 years. Women consult her about their relationships and parents allow her to 'adopt' their children. There'll be standing room only at her funeral!

Becoming a flirt ...

In this little book you will learn how to master the art of flirting. It contains everything you need to know to make yourself completely and utterly irresistible!

Great flirts love who they are and what they do. This book will help you discover how wonderful you are *and* encourage you to live your life from this position. It is about meeting yourself, falling in love with yourself and learning to interact with the world from that basis.

Think of this book as a guide, motivator and instigator of fun as you flirt your way through life.

Remember though, books don't jump out and change you overnight while you sleep. They offer you ways of thinking and acting that can help you to change yourself for the better. But you have to choose to do the work to make it happen!

Do you choose to become a great flirt? Let's start now!

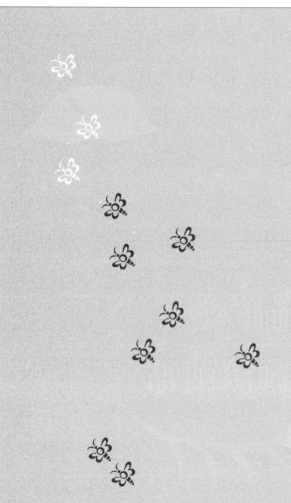

Are you a bit of
a flirt already?

As a successful flirt you will be able to make things happen *for* you, not *to* you. You will make things happen *because* of what you do, not *despite* what you do. What do you do now? You may have some patterns of behaviour that don't serve you and some that do. Let's look now at your current flirting patterns.

How do you currently flirt?

Perhaps you are a bit of a flirt already. Perhaps you flirt but don't get the results you want. Perhaps you don't flirt at all. The following questions will help you realize how flirtatious you currently are and what you need to work on:

are you a bit of a flirt already?

You are in a relaxed social situation and realize you are attracted to someone. Do you:

♥ Send out strong sexual signals and if they don't approach you, approach them?

♥ Flirt with someone else while occasionally looking in their direction?

♥ Hope that they don't notice you are interested and be certain to look away?

I was greeting people at the door of a seminar when a colleague arrived on the back of a taxi-bike. The rider came over to ask me more about the seminar. I thought he was gorgeous. After a short chat, I had to go. I handed him my card and started to walk downstairs. Halfway down I turned round and rushed back upstairs. I asked him if he would take me for a ride on his motorcycle. Two years later, we're still together!

Sometimes you have to follow your instincts and not worry about the consequences. I didn't stop to think this guy might refuse me or think I was too pushy – I just went for it!

are you a bit of a flirt already?

Sometimes you have to follow your
instincts and just go for it!

You are in a fairly well populated train carriage. A personable, well-presented person gets into the carriage and strikes up a conversation. Do you:

Ⓥ Say 'Good evening' and return to your paper or your work?

Ⓥ Ignore them – after all, they might be a bore or a rapist?

Ⓥ Open out to the possibilities and strike up a conversation?

Fran was directing a TV documentary about my seminar. On the train home, a man got into her carriage, smiled and said, '*Hello.*' Normally, Fran would have mumbled an indistinct greeting and got on with her work. This time, she remembered something I'd said about connecting, and she smiled back and made a comment about a topical event. They chatted and discovered they were both in the TV business *and* he knew her husband. They exchanged telephone numbers and made plans to meet up with their partners. Who knows where this friendship will lead?

Sometimes it is our willingness to take advantage of unlikely situations that leads us to a wonderful friendship, a new relationship or that great business opportunity.

are you a bit of a flirt already?

You know that someone you have met
recently but don't know too well could
connect you to someone who would be very
useful to you in your business. Do you:

- Ring up that person, ask them how they are,
  listen to what they say, make them feel good
  and then say honestly that you know they can
  help you and that's why you are calling?

- Ring them up about another matter and hope
  that one thing will lead to another?

- Stop yourself from calling because it would
  seem like using them?

Sue attended one of my personal development events. She called me up the next day, thanked me for the evening and then told me that she knew that I was an influential person and had a far wider reach in the personal development community than she did. She told me a story that made me laugh and asked if I would publicize her coaching. I attended one of her sessions and I did publicize her because she was good.

Sue was pro-active, funny and friendly. She had made me feel good without flattery and she was genuine and prepared to put herself on the line because she believed in herself.

Sometimes you have to be prepared
to put yourself on the line to make
a useful connection.

As a result of reading this, I suspect that you may have become more aware of how flirtatious you are. Would you like to initiate more conversations and be able to socialize in any situation? Have there been times in your life when you could have made a great connection, but didn't? If so, this book is for you.

are you a bit of a flirt already?

Beginning on the inside,
with yourself!

The secret to great flirting is to begin on the inside, with yourself! The better you know yourself and the more good you feel about yourself, the easier it is for you to flirt successfully and love it. Flirting is not just about the superficial outward displays, it starts with who you are shining through.

The key to successful flirting is to start out feeling good about yourself so that you can transmit this to others.

beginning on the inside, with yourself!

Do you know how wonderful you are?

Great flirts know who they are, rejoice in it and are honest about it. They feel good about themselves and convey that to others. If you want to be like this, it's important to know who you are and to be proud of it.

WHO ARE YOU?

What kind of person are you?

Write down what comes into your head when you read the question. Sense it and let it flow. Remember, when you are honest with yourself, there is no right or wrong, there is just what is . . .

To give you some idea, when I did this exploration myself I wrote quite a lot and here's some of it:

> *I am a person who loves animals. I write, I run groups and get a buzz from spending time with my cat, hanging out on the Internet and being with friends. I love coaching people to realize more of who they are. I am highly flirtatious and a voracious networker. I enjoy the time I spend with my lover and I love my own company. I like adventures and relish good food.*

Now reread what you wrote.

When you have finished reading this book, ask yourself this question again. You may find that you have discovered even more about the real you hiding beneath the layers we have peeled away . . .

beginning on the inside, with yourself!

Great flirts love who they are and what they do.

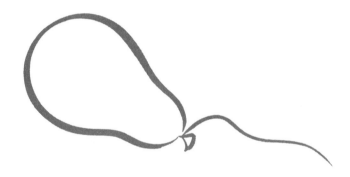

What do you really want?

Now you have defined who you are, you have to
know what you want, otherwise how will you know
if you've got it? Here's another exploration:

WHAT DO YOU REALLY, REALLY WANT?

Is there something you have been longing to
do? What are those big dreams, those deep
wishes and desires that you harbour deep
inside? If you were to wake up tomorrow and
find a miracle had happened, what would
your ideal life be like?

beginning on the inside, with yourself!

What do you want? Describe how it will be for you.

♥ Read what you have written.

♥ Now imagine everything you want being put into an enormous balloon and let it float away.

Why should you let go of what you want? It may seem strange, but once you know what you want and then let go of it, opportunities will open out for you. I don't know why, but people who continually worry about not getting what they want seem to struggle harder than those who just let go. Believe in your dreams and then get on with having a good time.

Simply the best

Flirting comes from being yourself at your best, loving yourself and giving out the glow of who you are.

What's true of you when you are at your best, completely and utterly?

You know because, for sure, at some time you have experienced those magical moments. When you recall how you are at your absolute best and begin to be like that more and more, that's when you become truly wonderful, splendid, abundant! You begin to have a sense of how you want your life to be. You attract the situations that are right for you. You flirt like crazy!

beginning on the inside, with yourself!

Building better beliefs

Our beliefs drive our actions. Great flirts live by green light *go-for-it* empowering beliefs. They believe they are desirable. They believe they are sexy. They believe they bring a little light into other people's lives and they believe other people are interesting. Less confident people are weakened by red light *stop-'em-dead* beliefs. If you believe you are not attractive, for instance, you will act as if you are not and you'll probably look less attractive to others.

I'm sure there are some juicy green light beliefs you'd like to have about yourself. Now's your chance to create and embody them. Here's how:

BEING YOUR BELIEF

- ⊙ Think of a belief you want to have about yourself.

- ⊙ Create a sentence that affirms that belief. Start with either of these two phrases:

    I can ...
    I am ...

- ⊙ Now say to yourself: *'When I am at my best, I can/am [your belief].'*

- ⊙ Now think of someone who has that belief about themselves or acts as if they believe something similar about themselves. For example, if you want to be more raunchy, Tina Turner might be a good role model.

beginning on the inside, with yourself!

- ⊙ Pay attention to how your role model stands, moves, breathes and acts.

- ⊙ Stand like that yourself – mimic the posture.

- ⊙ Say the belief to yourself over and over in your head.

- ⊙ Say your new belief out loud.

- ⊙ Continue to stand there for a while with the body stance of this new belief.

Repeat as necessary! The more you do this, the more your body takes on the cell memories of the belief and the more it appears as if it is true. Then one day it just is!

Great flirts live by empowering beliefs. They believe they are fun to be with, they believe they are sexy, and they believe they bring a little light into other people's lives.

beginning on the inside, with yourself!

Laughter, the best medicine

Great flirts spend more time laughing and smiling than other people. I'm sure you'll agree that a happy, laughing person is more attractive than a frowning misery. Furthermore, laughing releases opiates and endorphins, nature's happy drugs. When you laugh, you feel great!

Are you laughing enough? Find things that make you laugh. Watch TV programmes that make you laugh. Read books that make you laugh. Do things that make you laugh. Connect and spend time with people that make you laugh. Subscribe to a daily joke list. Go on a laughter workshop. Above all, learn to laugh at yourself.

Are you a 'sunshiner'?

I call people who give out the glow of their inner self 'sunshiners'. How do you react to life's challenges? Are you a sunshiner or a 'black clouder'?

⊙ Sunshiners look on the bright side.

⊙ Sunshiners see the funny side of any situation.

⊙ Sunshiners see people as an opportunity to connect.

⊙ Sunshiners notice what's good about others and tell them.

beginning on the inside, with yourself!

The Little Book of Flirting

⊙ Sunshiners face challenges with: 'How can I move on?' or 'What can I learn here?'

⊙ Sunshiners spend most of their time being who they are and loving it.

⊙ Sunshiners only notice the possibilities.

When you choose to be a shining sun, you'll find yourself giving out the glow of your own rays and that's one of the essentials of successful flirting.

Great flirts don't depend on other people to feel good, they create their own good times and spread them around!

beginning on the inside, with yourself!

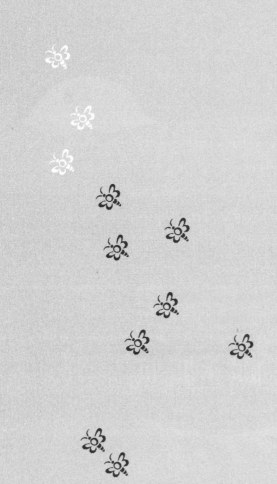

Sharpening up your senses

In order to become a successful flirt, you need to sharpen up your senses. Your senses are the media through which you pick up other people's signals. The more you can sense, the easier you will find it to flirt right on in there.

Great flirts have tuned up senses and are experts at unconsciously picking up small signals and 'tracking' the patterns of people they flirt with:

⊙ A good listener knows when a person has paused and takes up their cue to enter the conversation. They remember the words people use and play them back to them to help create rapport.

⊙ Someone with an eye for detail notices little changes in facial movement, skin tone or bodily gestures.

ⓥ A person who is in touch with their feelings
   often gets intuitive answers as to what move to
   make next.

Great flirts are able to sense another person's
reaction to them – they know when to move
more quickly or slowly – or, indeed, when
to stop and move on!

Using all the senses

I often go running along the seafront where I live.
Before starting my run, I decide which sense I want to
concentrate on developing. One day I pay special
attention to the sounds around me, the next I
concentrate on what I can see. This way I have really
begun to notice new things. I have also realized which
of my senses I need to sharpen up.

You can adapt the following exploration to your
everyday routine and do it as often as you like!

'SENSADAY' WORKOUT

Next time you go out alone for a walk or a run might be an ideal time to try this out.

DAY 1: VISION

You can begin by paying special attention to the sights around you. Describe what you see. Are there trees? What colour are their leaves? Look out for people, buildings, all the little details ...

DAY 2: SOUND

Today you can decide to spend some time concentrating on the sounds around you. When I go on my run, I am aware of the wind whistling, the sound of the ocean and the background noises of traffic. Keep your ears open and listen.

The Little Book of Flirting

sharpening up your senses

DAY 3: TOUCH AND FEELING

Concentrate on what you can feel. When the sun shines you may feel warmth. Perhaps you can feel the breeze or the texture of your clothes on your skin. This is an easy one to get to grips with once you start.

DAY 4: SMELL

Today you can concentrate on smell. When I run by the sea, I notice the smell of the sea, of the seaweed, of a cigarette as I pass by someone smoking and the different smells of the greenery.

DAY 5: TASTE

You can practise this exploration each time you eat a meal. Begin by saying to yourself that you are going to look for the taste of all the ingredients in whatever you are eating. Identify them. You might think that taste only works with edible objects, but later as you perk up your taste buds, you will begin to appreciate lots more tasty things.

When you continue to do this as a regular exploration and concentrate on different senses for a set amount of time each day, you will notice your senses becoming more acute and you will begin to notice more about the world around you and the people around you.

The sharper your senses, the easier you
will find it to flirt appropriately
and successfully.

The signals of flirting

If you want to become a superb flirt, it's important to
be aware of the signals people send out when they are
expressing interest – or not! You need to get two or
three clear and repeated signals before you can
interpret them as a potential 'come-on'.

Here are a few examples of signs that someone is
interested in you:

⊙ **brushing up against you and smiling**

⊙ **nodding their head whilst looking in your
direction**

ⓥ smiling broadly at you

ⓥ making repeated eye contact

ⓥ blinking slowly, looking up and sideways at you

ⓥ complimenting you

ⓥ dilating their pupils

ⓥ thrusting out their chest or breasts

ⓥ raising an eyebrow whilst looking at you

Here are some different signals, a mixture of which indicate that someone is probably *not* interested:

ⓥ one-time brief eye contact

ⓥ looking away

- (v) keeping the same posture

- (v) turning their body away from you

- (v) keeping their head vertical

- (v) normal or dull eyes

- (v) a closed mouth

- (v) sagging so as not to emphasize their breasts/chest

- (v) looking at someone else lustily!

This system isn't foolproof, however. People sometimes send out mixed signals. Don't take anything for granted. Be bold and go with your desires.

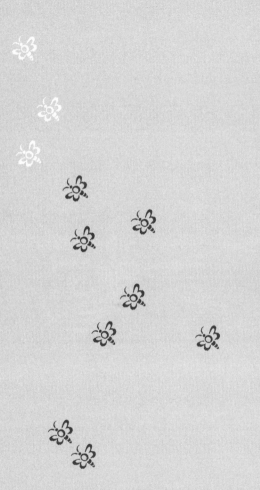

Friendly flirting

Friendly flirting is flirting with the sexuality turned
right down but not off. We are all sexual beings and
we shouldn't turn off what is natural or try to pretend
that we are not. BUT we can control the level of
sexuality we bring to interactions so that it is barely
perceptible and not offensive.

Friendly flirting shows you are confident, you have a
positive attitude AND you are a great person to have
around. The aim is to make people feel great about
themselves. It is about creating a fun atmosphere,
getting people to co-operate, radiating what is
wonderful about you, drawing people to you and
opening the channels for future opportunities.

Friendly flirting is a great way to shine a little
sunshine on everyone you meet.

friendly flirting

Great states are catching

I usually ask people in my flirting classes what they think would be a great state of mind to be in to flirt naturally and wonderfully. The most popular are feeling confident and playful.

What states of mind would put you in the mood for flirting? Pick a few. Here are some suggestions:

- Ⓥ sexy

- Ⓥ playful

- Ⓥ curious

- Ⓥ excited

- Ⓥ confident

- Ⓥ devil-may-care

- Ⓥ loving

Spend time remembering when you were like this. It recreates good feelings. Remember, people love to be around happy and confident people because their feel-good factor is infectious.

Friendly Flirting

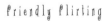

Smile, smile, smile ...

You may think this is obvious. Or is it? Have you noticed how many people just don't smile much? Are you one of those people who've become so serious they've forgotten how to have fun?

Great flirts will tell you that the more you smile, the more you are saying to the outside world, *'I am not a black cloud to be avoided, I am a sunshine person. Come bask in my rays ...'*

FAKE IT TILL YOU MAKE IT

You can start with a fake smile and it will eventually turn into a real one.

♥ Try it now. Just turn up the corners of your mouth and put on a smile ... Keep it going, make it wider. It doesn't matter if anyone is looking. Smile now!

♥ And pay attention to your body from head to toe. How are you sitting – are you comfortable? Is there anywhere in your body that is tense? Just noticing these things can help you to relax and release tension.

The Little Book of Flirting

Friendly Flirting

If you see someone without a smile,
give them one of yours!

Compliments – gifts from the heart

A genuine compliment costs nothing and it can light up someone's life. And once you make a person feel good, they're more likely to want to spend more time with you!

GIVING COMPLIMENTS

When I like someone or something about them, I tell them and this applies to friends, lovers and strangers. You can begin to do it too. Here are some things I have said to people:

'You did a great job.'

'Great smile / trainers / hair, etc.'

'You've got such a lovely energy.'

'You are so interesting.'

'What a lovely dog you have.'

'You are such a good listener, thanks!'

'You are so good at [whatever it is they are good at].'

'When I am with you I have so much fun.'

RECEIVING COMPLIMENTS

If you get a genuine compliment, doesn't it make sense to take it to heart! So how come we are so good at taking rejection to heart yet we tend to brush compliments over our shoulder?

Learn to accept a compliment with the grace and good feelings with which it was given. People who give genuine compliments do so because they appreciate something about you. So be proud of who you are and be proud that people are paying you compliments. Rejecting a compliment is like rejecting a gift.

Some good ways to receive compliments:

'Thank you, how nice of you to notice.'
'Thank you, it's one of my favourites.'
'Thank you, you've made my day.'

There are endless ways to receive a compliment, but it should always start with a smile and the words
'Thank you!'

Friendly Flirting

A compliment a day keeps the clouds away!

Be interesting by being interested

People like people who are interested in them. So quit trying to impress and concentrate on being impressed by them. Great flirts depend on their ability to get people to open up and talk (they are experts in make-'em-chat lines!). Everyone loves to talk about themselves because it makes them feel valuable and interesting.

The best questions you can ask are the ones that lead someone to remember a positive experience. You could start by offering a short sentence on how you like to have fun, relax, etc, and then ask them ...

The Little Book of Flirting

Friendly Flirting

⊙ 'What's your ideal way to have fun?'

⊙ 'How do you like to relax?'

⊙ 'Tell me about your best holiday ever.'

⊙ 'What are you passionate about?'

⊙ 'If you could wake up tomorrow and have it all, what would your ideal day be like?'

CAUTION: Don't turn into an interrogator. Just remember to make sure you spend at least 60% of the time listening to THEM!

friendly flirting

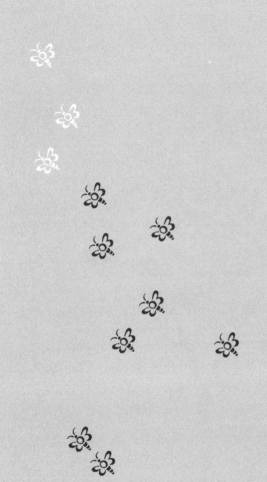

Sexual flirting

Sexual flirting is an inbuilt biological mechanism designed to help us attract a mate. It sends out definite sexual signals, such as *'I'm interested in you in a sexual way, how about you?'* It's great for initiating sex, keeping the flame lit and turning up the heat.

This kind of flirting isn't just for singletons looking for love. Flirting wantonly or even coyly with your partner while reminding them of wicked, wonderful times you've shared will cause them to fantasize about what is to come.

So, if you want it, this is how to go for it!

Sexuality is not just about body friction and orgasms.
It is an energy that runs through us, constantly driven
by the primitive biological instinct to mate. We are all
deeply sexual beings and yet we have learned to
sometimes suppress our sexuality and even feel
embarrassed by it. How much better might your
attitude to your sexuality be if you had been taught
to enjoy it with passion and pride?

Awakening and enjoying your sexuality doesn't mean
using your sexual energy to get what you want. It is
about enjoying your sexuality to increase your
wellbeing and natural flirtatiousness, and make your
life more vibrant and juicy!

sexual flirting

The more comfortable you are with being and
feeling sexy, the more you will come across
as a sexually attractive person.

Send out multiple signals

People have preferences for different mediums of
signalling. Some notice looks, some notice touch, and
others pick up words and sounds.

On page 53 we looked at what sort of signals people
send out when they are expressing interest in you.
Now it's your turn! Be sure to communicate your
interest in all three mediums to increase your chances
of sending a clear signal. Show you like them with
prolonged eye contact, a broad smile and preening
gestures. Say something to them that indicates you are
interested – a compliment works well here. And, if you
get a chance, use touch gently, such as accidentally
brushing up against them. Notice which signals they
respond to best and adapt your behaviour accordingly.

sexual flirting

Juicy voices have more fun

The voice is one of nature's most powerful flirting
tools, and great flirts generally give great voice!
Sound doesn't just go in via our ears, it hits our body
with sound waves. Sometimes they can be wonderful;
sometimes they are painful. Voices create feelings in
other people. Think of the possibilities.

There are some people whose voices just seem to
ooze sexuality in their juicy rich tones. Wouldn't it be
useful to be able to speak like this sometimes?

The following exploration is designed to juice up
your voice, so be sure to go for it!

JUICING UP YOUR VOICE

Find somewhere where you won't be disturbed to do this.

Think of a time when you had a really juicy moment in your life and say the following 'words' with as much meaning as possible:

- 'Ooooooooooh!' (Something juicy has just been presented to you.)

- 'Aaaaaaaah ...' (You are sighing with relief, as when getting into a warm bath after a long day.)

- 'Mmmmmm.' (You are deeply excited by a new prospect.)

sexual flirting

The Little Book of Flirting

⊙ 'Yes pleeeeeaaaaaseee!' (You want something
   so badly you are begging for it!)

Do this often. Vary the tone, rhythm, speed
and volume. Experiment and have fun flexing
your voice.

Great flirts give great voice!

Move that body

Your body is another powerful flirting instrument.
Great flirts are generally great movers!

Dancing is a wonderful way to free up your body, so
you become more relaxed and able to let go and flirt
naturally. Dancing can be done alone or with others.
It can be done to strict steps or it can be freeform. It is
a great form of self-expression and a way of
interacting with someone else ... and deepening the
connection. And dancing is sexy. Great flirts entice
others with their sensual movements!

Take every opportunity to dance as freely, as often and as flexibly as you need to become a superb mover. It can be a hulu or ceroc or merengue, salsa, tango – anything, as long as it gets you to move and sway in a sexy way. Join a class, check out the local directories, hire or buy a video, mimic dancing on TV! It will open you up and you meet people at dancing classes!

Keep the pilot light burning

We are mostly taught that sexual arousal must be followed by orgasm. Generally when we experience sexual arousal at times that might be inappropriate to follow it through, we respond by contracting our energy and repressing the desire. It is the repression that leads to frustration. But you can learn to get mildly 'turned on' and turn it into a sensually motivating force which can be used in many situations!

Think of your sexual energy as the pilot light in your boiler. It's a real fiddle to relight if it goes out. When it just burns there with a flickering flame, it is ready to spring into roaring action. The pilot light exists to save you the trouble of relighting the boiler each time you want heating or hot water. When you turn on the tap, it heats up instantly!

PRACTISE YOUR WAY TO ECSTASY

When you continue to do this on a regular basis you will find yourself becoming more easily aroused and able to generate sexual energy to create a variety of feelings, from just feeling nice and juicy to passionate desire. Then you can choose whether you want to send out a strong sexual vibration or a mild one!

CONTINUING TO ENJOY THE EXPERIENCE

When you have practised this on your own at home and have gained the necessary delicate control of taking yourself to a gentle state of excitement without getting full blown arousal, you may find it is something you can generate in other situations. Men may have to practise a little longer to find that 'just before it gets embarrassing' point whereas women can do it anywhere without drawing undue attention to themselves. All that people will notice is that you have a little bit more of a shine in your eyes and a flush on your cheeks and that you are glowing more!

◉ Imagine you have a pilot light in your hara point (a spot about two inches below your navel which is considered to be the centre of your sexual energy) and think sexy.

(v) As you become mildly aroused, notice where the feelings are strongest.

(v) Breathe into that place as you inhale, imagine the pilot light expanding into full flame and spreading the resultant energy to all of your body, filling you with joy and smiles.

(v) As you exhale, imagine turning the pilot light down as the feelings subside until a small flame of energy remains flickering.

When you practise this regularly, you can experience exquisite moments and even mild orgasmic feelings from time to time.

Always keep your sexual energy bubbling and the pilot light lit.

Turning your sexual meter up and down

Your body can generate sexual energy at will or unconsciously. Imagine that your body is a boiler with a thermostatic meter and a pilot light. The meter measures sexual energy on a scale of 0 to 5: 0 is turned off, 1 is just bubbling under and 5 is all fired up and ready for hot sex!

When the pilot light is lit (see exploration on page 86) and on level 1, the process of turning the heat up or down is a simple one.

The Little Book of Flirting

sexual flirting

ADJUSTING YOUR SEXUAL ENERGY

Sex is a wonderful and exciting part of our natural life. We should always respect the presence of our sexuality in any encounter and moderate it accordingly. When you are flirting for sex, turn up that meter to no. 5 (think sexy thoughts and imagine your sexual energy flowing round your body, filling you with desire). When you are flirting to attract someone but don't want sex straightaway, you should moderate your sexual energy, so only turn it up a little bit, say to no. 3. And when you are flirting professionally to make someone feel good, turn it to no. 1.5, which is just enough to add that edge to your encounter without being overtly sexual.

Some people give off too much sexual energy too often and inappropriately, other don't give off enough sexual energy. Some have turned it off altogether!

(See *The 6 Don'ts of Flirting* section for more about this.) When you have smooth flowing, adjustable sexual energy you will become a very polished flirt, because you will be giving out just the right amount of sexual energy for the situation.

sexual flirting

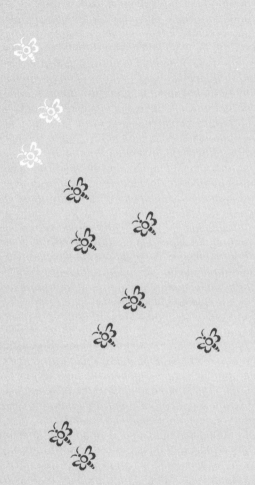

Social events –
giving out the glow

Being able to flirt with people at social events is great for building positive connections that other people want to continue. You can flirt with a lot of people briefly and still manage to set the scene for further contact or an invitation.

When you radiate and spread your inner glow to other people, you can begin to develop a deep energetic rapport and your connections will be more fun and rewarding.

Great flirts radiate what is wonderful about them to everyone they meet.

Eye to eye

When eyes meet, a spark is ignited which can be put out instantly or fanned into a fiercely burning fire. Eye contact is such an important part of the mating ritual that humans are almost the only primates that have the facility to mate face to face.

Our eyes are one of our most powerful signalling mechanisms. If you are going to connect successfully with someone, whether it is romantic or social, you have to make eye contact.

MORE EYE CONTACT

If you tend to look away from people rather than make eye contact, try this out.

When you are walking down the street next time (in a safe, busy, daylight environment if you are a woman), try making eye contact with as many people as possible. Set yourself a target of three a day and build it up by one more each day.

When you notice someone you like, force yourself to make eye contact. You can easily walk away, but just get into the habit of looking at people you like. You'd be surprised how many people tell me that they avoid eye contact with people they are attracted to and end up flirting with people that they aren't interested in!

Surveying the scene

We know that deep eye contact can convey deep feelings, but that's not always immediately appropriate. I'm sure you've been in situations where you needed to have a look around and survey the scene before making a move, with your eyes or otherwise! Here are a few ways to do this elegantly and quietly.

- ♥ When you want to survey a room, try looking just at the top of people's heads. You will get a peripheral view of everyone and they won't know you're looking at them in particular.

- ♥ When you want to survey an individual, imagine there is a circle round their face and run your eyes round the edge of that circle. You won't be making eye contact directly and they won't know what you're up to.

- ♥ You can also defocus your eyes and look behind someone, which enables you to get an impression of them without making direct eye contact.

social events – giving out the glow

Taking it further

When you spot someone you want to get friendlier with, you can use longer eye contact with a smile to say '*Hi, hello, I'm here.*' Even longer eye contact says '*Hi, hello, I'm here. I'm interested!*' A few repeated eye contacts will drive the message home!

Eye contact is a vital communication opener,
but eye contact coupled with a smile is an
even more powerful flirting tool.

Forget the chat up and make them chat

When people ask me for great chat-up lines, I always reply that the best is simply '*Hello*' or '*Hi*'. Then, after the initial contact, you can get the person to open up and talk by asking questions (see page 69 for some great make-'em-chat lines!) – everyone loves to talk about themselves! When you first meet someone, you will communicate more through the way you feel and the energy you exude than through any fancy words you can come up with.

If chat-up lines work, it's usually because the people using them feel great enough about themselves to take the risk. They are their own lines. You can be, too. You don't need anything else.

Great flirts don't depend on clever chat-up lines or having something meaningful to say. They depend on their ability to get people to open up and talk.

No, next!

If you don't get a positive response when you approach a person, never mind – someone out there is waiting for your glow to settle on them, so keep at it.

One of the things I advise all my students is that 'no' can be a signal to either try a different approach or move on to someone else. I am constantly reminding them: '*When you get a "no", go on to the next.*' No, next, no, next! Bingo! Yes!

social events - giving out the glow

Creating instant
rapport

Have you ever experienced a situation where you just seemed to hit it off with someone and the interaction flowed? You might also have had moments when you just couldn't seem to relate to someone. If you do get on with someone very easily, the chances are you have a deep natural rapport with them.

How much more powerful will a flirtatious encounter be when you discover and use tested methods of creating an instant rapport in situations where it might not happen naturally?

WHAT DO I MEAN BY 'RAPPORT'?

Rapport is defined in the dictionary as 'a harmonious social interaction'. I see it as a dance between two or even more people with a flow of communication both verbally and non-verbally. It is also a shared rhythm and way of moving.

Great flirts know how to create a deep rapport in situations where it might not happen naturally.

CREATE ONLY GOOD MAGIC

Before we start, a word of warning. Some people have tried using rapport skills to manipulate people in ways that are not useful to them or others. This might work initially, but it will also wear off quickly and when it does, the people who were manipulated will not like whoever tried it and in the end that person will feel bad as well. And I know you only want to influence others by making them feel good.

Awareness is all

People are giving you information every second you are with them, even from across a room. Like a warrior you need to be alert to what is going on and be ready to act rapidly when you get the signal.

As you start to really notice people, you will begin to pick up on the unique things they do:

⊙ You will notice how they change their physiology to match their mood.

⊙ You will notice the rate of and changes in their breathing.

creating instant rapport

⊙ You will notice the type of descriptive language they use according to the way they sense the world.

⊙ You will realize that when people do these things they are giving you a holographic map of their experience. What treasures do you think a map like that might show to you?

The two most powerful ways to gain rapport with someone are to breathe at the same rate as them and to match their energy levels. Naturally I don't advise you do this with someone who is very depressed, drunk or out of control!

Matching breathing

You know how an animal sniffs out the air, opening
its nostrils and parting its lips, checking out the
sounds and smells? You can do all this and more. You
can notice many things through your peripheral
vision and you can catch the rise and fall of
someone's breathing and allow yourself to just fall
into the same rhythm and breathe along with them ...

BREATHE ...

Try this on the train or bus. Pick someone to experiment with and look around (not directly at) their shoulders and upper chest. You will probably notice the rise and fall of their jacket or their shoulders. This is a clue to their breathing rate. Keeping your eyes on the breathing cues, start breathing in time with them.

When you do this exploration with strangers, nothing will happen unless you decide to make eye contact and interact with them. It's entirely safe!

Breathing at the same pace as someone is one of the most powerful ways to deepen an encounter with them.

Sensing their energy

You know that everyone has different energy levels. If you can match someone's energy comfortably, you will gain instant rapport with them.

So, before you approach a person, watch them for a while and notice how they move. People show their energy levels in the way they move. Ask yourself these questions as you watch them:

ⓥ **Are their movements rapid and jerky?**

ⓥ **Are they rhythmical and flowing?**

ⓥ Are they speedy and light?

ⓥ Are they solid and slow?

As you watch the person, imagine yourself making similar movements. This is a form of mental rehearsal. It makes it easy to just take on someone else's movement pattern.

Slowly, ease your body into the sense of the person's movement and get a sense of their rhythm and their flow.

When you get a sense of their rhythm and begin to synchronize with them, you will already have established deep rapport without saying a word and you will be in a position to lead them to an energy level that is right for both of you.

creating instant rapport

Tonal rapport

Another great way to get into synch with someone is to match their tone or speed of voice.

You can start by just noticing the speed of their voice and then matching it. If they are talking too fast or too slowly for you, once you have matched their level, you can gently slow down or speed up a little. Provided you do it at a comfortable pace, bit by bit, you will be able to bring them and yourself to a mid level that is comfortable for *both* of you.

When you match a person at their level they feel comfortable and they like you, because people like people who are like themselves.

creating instant rapport

Respecting their space

When you enter someone's personal space you might do so as a welcome guest or an alien invader or a bold visitor who believes they can just pop in. Are you a space invader?

As you stand and talk to people every day in the normal course of your life, begin to notice the 'language' of space.

☉ When you get close, do they move backwards, even minutely?

☉ Are they trying to change sides all the time?

⊙ Do they start to fidget as you get closer?

⊙ Do they contract a bit, bringing their arms in or crossing their arms?

⊙ Do they put their hands up as if to push you away?

These are all signs that you are TOO CLOSE!

Before you blunder in you've got to learn to case their space. When you approach strangers, test their personal space by moving closer slowly as you notice their reactions (such as slight changes in facial movements, eyes narrowing or changes in breathing rate). When you sense the changes, stop or move back slowly to remove the threat.

Talking their language

We all use a rich variety of sensory language based on the senses of sight, sound, touch/feeling, smell and taste. Most of us, however, have our preferences and we give out loads of clues to these preferences. The words people use often reveal through which sense, or mixture of senses, they primarily experience the world. Pay attention to what they say.

Here are a few examples:

VISION

'Things seem to be blown out of all proportion.'

'I wish I could shed some light on this.'

'I see what you mean.'

'I take a dim view of your activities.'

SOUND

'We are definitely on the same wavelength.'

'That sounds good to me.'

'I got it loud and clear.'

'What you said definitely rings a bell with me.'

TOUCH/FEELING

'He's a really slimy character.'

'Let's keep in touch.'

'I can feel it in my water.'

'I'm out of sorts.'

creating instant rapport

So, next time you have a conversation with someone, make a point of keeping your ears open for the type of sensory language they use. Pay attention to what they prefer and when you get a sense of it, start using those kinds of words back to them. Great flirts instinctively pick up on other people's language and use it in their conversation so that the person they are engaging feels comfortable with them.

Deep rapport - bubbling up

When you enter the dance and go with the flow and the rhythm, whether in a group of people or with someone you desire, you will begin to be able to incorporate all this into your own potent mixture of who you are at your best, mingling and communicating with other people, glowing as you dance the dance of deep rapport, drawing them closer to you.

Great flirts dance the dance of deep rapport, creating instant harmony and accord, and drawing people closer to them.

creating instant rapport

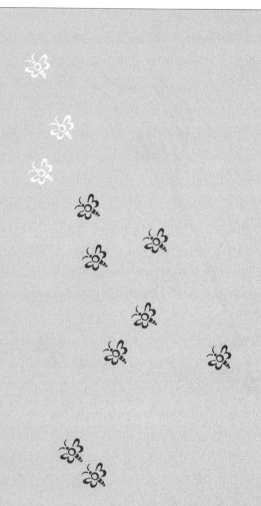

The 6 don'ts
of flirting

1. Don't take life too seriously

Geri, a successful advertising executive, felt she had had to fight her way to her current position. She was good at what she did and in her own words she '*didn't tolerate fools*'. She had been passed over for an account directorship which had gone to Adele, a woman whom Geri considered frivolous. When pressed, Geri admitted that Adele was a brilliant account executive, but she thought she spent too much time 'fooling around'. Geri equated success with being tough and serious. She thought that she had to suppress her feminine qualities in order to succeed.

Geri realized that if she had allowed herself to have more fun, she might have been more popular. When she asked a colleague what Adele had that she didn't, she was told: *'Adele is like a ray of sunshine. She's so easy to work with because she makes everything seem like fun.'* Geri learnt the hard way that having fun and success in business are compatible.

2. Don't use your sexuality inappropriately or unfairly

Rachel confessed to me that her great flirting secret was to *'think about dirty sex, stare at someone and if they don't react, pull them towards me.'* *'The only trouble'*, she whined, *'is that they all want sex and all I want most of the time is a drink.'*

Rachel was a classic sexual flirt. She thought the only way she could attract the attention of a man was to promise sex. So she turned it on full blast and then wondered why men always made a grab for her.

WHAT'S THE MESSAGE HERE?

Sexuality is a primary driving force in all humans. We can use it beautifully and exquisitely when the time is right to draw someone to us. There are also times when it isn't appropriate or fair to flirt sexually.

The Little Book of Flirting

the 6 don'ts of flirting

3. Don't be scared of your sexuality

Naomi, on the other hand, was terrified of flirting for fear of the reaction it would cause. She went out once with a man she quite liked and when they kissed, he got an erection. Naomi ran a mile! She was scared of the power of her sexuality and she saw the man's reaction as a sign that he was bound to expect sex.

WHAT'S THE MESSAGE HERE?

Somewhere along the line someone had told Naomi that men were uncontrollable animals and women must temper their behaviour so as not to arouse their animal instincts.

When Naomi learnt to feel good about herself, she also learnt to accept that it is natural for men to be sexually attracted to women. Instead of seeing herself as a wicked temptress, she was grateful that she was a sexy desirable woman.

the 6 don'ts of flirting

4. Don't forget you are a sexual being

Chris was Mr Nice. He always ended up as a friend but never the boyfriend. He had no problem asking women out, but he never got as far as taking the relationship to a more sexual level. He spent so much time being Mr Nice he forgot how to be Mr Sexy. Women like a mixture of both!

WHAT'S THE MESSAGE HERE?

Chris learned that he could turn up his sexual meter a little and send different messages to women.

5. Don't be scared to show someone you like them

Leanne was quite good at flirting – with the wrong men. If she liked someone she wouldn't flirt with them for fear of being rejected. Instead she flirted with people who seemed interested in her. She flirted herself into a string of 'wrong' relationships ending in an unhappy marriage and a nasty divorce.

WHAT'S THE MESSAGE HERE?

Leanne learned that she needed to go for what she wanted instead of what she thought was her lot.

6. Don't forget how wonderful you are

Lisa came into daily contact with powerful and famous people as part of her work. When she was at work and was one to one with people she felt great and 'in control', but when she had to go to socialite parties, she suddenly dried up. Everyone in the room seemed more important, more interesting and more fun than her.

Lisa felt good when she had the backup of her work to give her status. Once she was no longer in control, she lost her confidence. She built up pictures of people rejecting her overtures or finding her

conversation boring. Lisa's mother had always
pointed out lively people at parties and called them
'show offs' ...

WHAT'S THE MESSAGE HERE?

Lisa learned to love herself more and to expect others
to value her company and opinions. She learned to
'flirt with life'.

A final word

Now is the time to set free your flirtatious self and really go for what you want. There is a whole world out there waiting to help you fulfil those great big dreams.

Thank you for taking the time to read this book. I encourage you to continue to learn and look for ways to develop yourself personally. You only have one life and it is happening now. Remember to be how you are at your best at all times and go out there and flirt for whatever you want *right now*!

Be who you are and love who you are and you will find yourself connecting at the right time with people who are right for you.

a final word

Peta Heskell and the flirting academy

If you like this book and you sense you want more, you might benefit from some coaching or by attending one of the Flirting Academy courses. Peta Heskell can coach you on all aspects of flirting, confidence, dating and mating. Coaching is available as one-to-one sessions or by telephone and e-mail.

The Flirting Academy runs one-day and weekend flirting 'play' shops, facilitated by Peta, in London and abroad to help people have more fun, become more confident and improve their communication skills. Tailored training is available for the corporate market.

If you want to know more, pick up the phone or get online!

WEBSITE: **www.flirtcoach.com**
E-MAIL: **info@flirtcoach.com**
TELEPHONE: **+ 44 (0) 700 4 354 784**

Flirt Coach *by Peta Heskell*

Communication tips for Friendship, Love and Professional Success

Peta Heskell has refined flirting to a fine art – one that can be used not just in romantic relationships but in every relationship (with teachers, neighbours, clients and so on) to make communication more fun. Peta insists that the key to successful socializing and relationships is being able to be yourself. She offers a straightforward programme to help anyone learn to be comfortable with being themselves. As she sees it, flirting can be the key to success, in every sphere.

Her system works by:

- looking at the inside – finding out what is really you, your belief system and reviving your innate skills of childlike curiosity, daring and intuition.
- looking at the outside – learning how to understand people's signals and how to get your message across. How to 'glow', how to wield power and influence.
- application: specific ways to apply her flirting techniques for career, friendship and love.

Peta Heskell is a Master NLP practitioner and has led workshops for more than ten years. She offers workshops throughout the UK as well as one-to-one coaching sessions.

ISBN 0-00-710843-5
Order a copy now at www.thorsons.com

The Flirt Coach's Guide to Love and Romance *by Peta Heskell*

Communication tips for relationship bliss

A guide to perfecting your flirting skills, from Flirt Coach Peta Heskell. Use your communication skills to get exactly what you want in love, sex and relationships.

Peta Heskell has refined flirting to a fine art – a sexy, lighthearted art that makes communication fun and has the power to transform your romantic relationships. Successful flirts draw people to them with ease and once they have got that special someone's attention, they rarely lose it!

Peta insists that the key to successful relationships is being able to be yourself. She offers a straightforward programme to help anyone learn to be comfortable with being themselves. As she sees it, flirting can be the key to success in love, life and especially in the bedroom!

Peta Heskell is a Master NLP practitioner and has led workshops for more than ten years. She offers workshops throughout the UK as well as one-to-one coaching sessions.

ISBN 0-00-714767-8
Order a copy now at www.thorsons.com